MADE IN
ANCIENT GREECE

MADE IN ANCIENT GREECE

by Christine Price

Illustrated with photographs
and drawings

NEW YORK

E. P. DUTTON & CO., INC.

ALSO BY CHRISTINE PRICE

Made in the Middle Ages
Made in the Renaissance
The Story of Moslem Art

This book is for Foukaina
because it is about her country

Αὐτό τό βιβλίο εἶναι διά τήν
Φουκαῖνα διότι ἀναφέρει τά τῆς
Πατρίδος της

CONTENTS

III Athens and the Classical Age

IV To the Ends of the Earth

AUTHOR'S NOTE

I am grateful to the following museums for providing me with photographs and permitting me to include them in my book:

The Trustees of the British Museum, London; the Metropolitan Museum of Art, New York; the Museum of Fine Arts, Boston; the Royal Ontario Museum, University of Toronto; and the Wadsworth Atheneum, Hartford, Connecticut.

For additional photographs I would like to thank Miss Evalyn A. Clark, Poughkeepsie, New York; the Greece News Bureau, New York; the United Arab Republic Tourist Office, New York; and also the Art Reference Bureau, Ancram, New York, who spared no effort to find exactly the pictures I needed.

I am especially grateful to Miss Elizabeth Chase of the Yale University Art Gallery for reading and criticizing my manuscript.

In attempting to write about Greek art, I naturally found the most valuable experience was a visit to Greece to see the art of the Greeks in its proper setting; but I also owe a great debt to many authors who have written brilliantly about the ancient Greeks and their art. Out of the countless books on Ancient Greece, I have listed on my last page a few recent ones that I found immensely helpful and interesting. Most of them have fine illustrations, and they often contain lists of other books for deeper exploration into the story of Greek art.

I hope that my book, serving as an introduction to a subject so vast and exciting, may also be an invitation to readers to make their own discoveries of the delights of Greek art, not only through books and in museums, but perhaps in the wonderful land of Greece itself.

C. P.

Massalia

CORSICA

SARDINIA

ADRIATIC SEA

Rome
ITALY
Tarentum

SICILY
Gela Syracuse

Carthage

MACEDONIA

ATTICA
PELOPONNESE

MEDITERRANEAN SEA

THRACE

Byzantium
SAMOTHRACE

Troy

Pergamum
Cyme

IONIA
Ephesus

RHODES

CRETE

CYPRUS

BLACK SEA

Panticapaeum

SEA OF
MARMARA

ASIA MINOR

Antioch

Sidon
Tyre

Cyrene

Alexandria

Jerusalem

Naucratis
(Greek
settlement)

EGYPT

River Nile

RED SEA

Luxor

Mount
Olympus

Artemisium

ITHACA Delphi Tanagra
Athens

Corinth
ELIS
Olympia

Sparta

IONIAN
SEA

AEGEAN
SEA

Piraeus
Sunium
SALAMIS
DELOS

SIPHNOS

GREECE

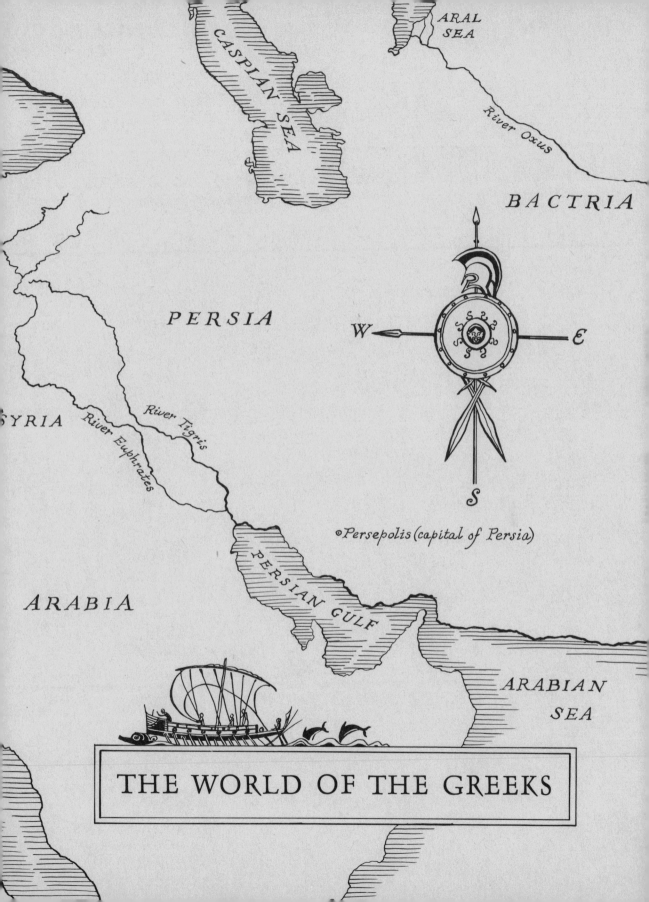

ARAL SEA

CASPIAN SEA

River Oxus

BACTRIA

PERSIA

W

E

S

SYRIA

River Euphrates

River Tigris

⊙Persepolis (capital of Persia)

ARABIA

PERSIAN GULF

ARABIAN SEA

THE WORLD OF THE GREEKS

I THE GREEKS AND
THEIR WORLD

THE PARTHENON FROM
THE NORTHWEST

ANIMALS, MEN AND GODS

High on a rocky hill, in the middle of the city of Athens, stands the Parthenon, the mighty temple of the goddess Athena. Its marble columns, pale golden in the sunshine, rise from a platform built of massive blocks of stone. The temple is roofless now, and the sun streams down on the bare paving within, where the great statue of Athena once stood; but outside, above the tops of the columns, you can still see fragments of wonderful marble sculptures, the work of Greek stone-carvers more than two thousand years ago.

Many of the sculptures from the Parthenon were taken away to England at the beginning of the nineteenth century to save them from destruction, for the ruined temple was not cared for then as it is today. The "Elgin marbles"—named

Above A PRANCING HORSE FROM THE FRIEZE OF THE PARTHENON

after Lord Elgin who had brought them to England—were put in the British Museum, and they soon became so famous that people thought that all Greek art in ancient times consisted of marble sculptures and magnificent temples like the Parthenon.

Yet long before the fifth century B.C., when the Parthenon was built, there had been fine artists and craftsmen in Greece, men who worked in bronze and clay, gold, silver and ivory, as well as stone. Their art looks very different from the sculptures of the Parthenon, but the subjects they chose for statues or paintings were the same, and they looked at their world with the same delight. The old Greek word for statue means "delight," and the art of the ancient Greeks was full of joy.

12

RACING
CHARIOT

The artists lead us into a world of animals, men and gods.

Animals were important to the Greeks as the friends—or the enemies—of man. They had a special love for horses, their companions in war and sport, and the sculptors of the Parthenon were not the only artists to take delight in portraying horses and riders or a swift chariot drawn by a prancing team.

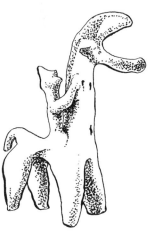

HORSES AND
RIDERS

THE HUNTER'S
RETURN

Dogs were good friends of man, faithful guardians and
hunters; and wild animals, too, had their place in Greek art.
The heroes of Greece tested their strength in fights with lions,
boars and serpents. Mythical centaurs, half horse and half

MAN ATTACKING
A WILD BOAR

man, were said to roam among the mountains; they often appeared in paintings and sculptures, and artists also portrayed other fantastic creatures, such as sphinxes and gorgons, sometimes comic and sometimes terrible.

But it was man who stood at the center of the world. To the Greeks, people were the most exciting and beautiful subjects for an artist to paint or carve.

GALLOPING
CENTAUR

15

In Greek art we meet all kinds of people. There are shepherds and seafarers, warriors, athletes and singers of songs, and above all, there are the heroes of myth and legend, whose adventures were chanted by Greek storytellers. The heroes possessed almost godlike strength and courage and pride. The Greeks loved the stories of the Labors of Herakles and his epic battles with savage beasts; of Theseus, the slayer of the Minotaur; of Jason who sailed forth in his ship, the *Argo,* in quest of the Golden Fleece; and of Achilles and the heroes of the Trojan War whose tale was told by Homer in *The Iliad.*

Because the Greeks found people so fascinating, and admired so much the beauty of the human body, it was natural that they should think of the gods as strong and beautiful men and women. The goddesses must be serenely lovely, and the gods modeled after the Greek athletes, the champions of the games.

16

WARRIOR FROM
SPARTA

THESEUS SLAYING
THE MINOTAUR

The Greeks believed in many gods. The chief of them was Zeus, lord of the sky, the lightning and the thunder. Hera was the wife of Zeus, and Athena, the goddess of wisdom and of handicrafts, was one of his daughters. She was known as the Maiden—*Parthenos*—and she usually carried a spear and wore the helmet and breastplate of a warrior.

17

COMIC ACTOR

In this painting we see the miraculous birth of Athena, who leaps, fully armed, from the forehead of Zeus, as he sits enthroned with a thunderbolt in his hand. Ares, god of war, is looking on at the right, with a terrible gorgon-head painted on his shield, while Hermes, messenger of the gods, stands at the left, in his hat and winged boots. Behind the throne is Apollo with his lyre—the god of musicians and poets and the bringer and healer of sickness, both in body and mind.

Apollo was also the god of light and of the sun, while his twin sister, Artemis, was the moon-goddess. She ruled over the wild beasts and was the patron of hunters.

18

EROS WITH A FAN

DIONYSOS WITH
GRAPEVINES

Aphrodite, the gentle goddess of beauty, was another daughter of Zeus, and her small son Eros was the god of love. Demeter ruled over the earth and the farmers' fields of corn, while Poseidon, the brother of Zeus, ruled the sea and had the power to stir up the earthquakes that still are an ever-present danger in Greece.

Dionysos was the god of wine and merrymaking and the patron of the theater. His friends were the satyrs, cheerful creatures with pointed ears and bushy beards, snub noses and long horses' tails.

19

The craftsmen's own god was lame Hephaistos, the smith, the patron of all men who worked in metal. Homer tells in *The Iliad* how Hephaistos, with immortal skill, made a shield and armor for the legendary hero, Achilles.

HEPHAISTOS
IN HIS WORKSHOP
MAKING ACHILLES'
SHIELD

Like men, the gods were not always at peace with one another. They were as hot-tempered and loving, fickle and wily as the Greeks themselves, and they took a keen interest in men's affairs. They often traveled far and wide to help their

20

favorites or to strike down their enemies. A man whom the gods favored was fortunate indeed, but it went hard with him if he offended them.

After the fall of Troy, as Homer describes it, the victorious Greeks angered the sea-god Poseidon, who lashed their ships with terrible storms on their way home to Greece. The hero Odysseus suffered longest of all. He lost his ship and all his men, and it was only with the help of Athena that he finally reached his home on the island of Ithaca after ten years of wanderings and wild adventures.

GREEK WARSHIP

Odysseus, like all Greeks, had a deep love for his own land, the place where he was born. The Greeks believed that even the gods had homes to return to, not in some remote heaven, but in the land of Greece. Zeus and his family were said to dwell on the cloudy peak of Mount Olympus in northern Greece. The gods and goddesses also had their own holy places where temples had been built in their honor; and cities were placed under their protection, as Athens was protected by Athena in her magnificent temple, the Parthenon.

The gods of the ancient Greeks were as strongly rooted in the land as the men who worshiped them.

21

THE LAND OF GREECE

Greece is a harsh, craggy country of high mountains and deep valleys, where the sea is never very far away.

In the Gulf of Corinth the sea bites into the land, almost splitting the country in two, and cutting off the northern part of Greece from the south, the Peloponnese. Today, as in ancient times, travelers coming from the Peloponnese to the Shrine of Apollo at Delphi see a shoreline of majestic mountains, as they sail northward across the Gulf. Dominating the range is the great rocky mass of Mount Parnassus, the home of the Muses, the goddesses of poetry, song and dance. The Shrine of

Above DELPHI
FROM THE GULF
OF CORINTH

VIEW FROM DELPHI OVER THE OLIVE GROVES TO THE PORT OF ITEA

Apollo, who ruled over the Muses, is set upon the mountain's southern slope, where a sacred spring gushes out between the mighty cliffs.

23

WOMAN
SPINNING

To the Greeks, the high, wild places were fitting homes for the gods. Men settled in the valleys below, where they could plow the earth and plant wheat and vineyards and groves of gray-green olive trees.

Here, among the fields, little towns grew up, communities of merchants and craftsmen with market places in which goods were bought and sold. The towns were cut off from one another by the mountain ranges, and the townspeople were always ready to defend themselves against their neighbors in the next valley. Each town had its acropolis—"high city"—a rocky hill that could be used as a stronghold in time of attack.

Men were fiercely loyal to their own cities, and there was often bitter rivalry between the small separate "city-states." The Greeks loved town life, the crowds and noise and endless discussions of politics, and they expected all free men to take an active part in city government.

In Athens, the center for political arguments and for buying and selling was the Agora, the great market place in the shadow of the Acropolis. Athens was a small city in ancient times, and the valley where it lay was green with farms and vineyards. Today, if you stand on the Acropolis, close by the Parthenon, you see the valley filled with houses, but the mountains above it have not changed. Shepherds still keep their flocks on the bare ridges as they did centuries ago, and bees still collect nectar from the spicy mountain flowers to make the famous Greek honey.

DANCING BEFORE THE ALTAR OF A GOD

THE HEART OF ATHENS: THE ACROPOLIS AT THE RIGHT, THE AGORA IN THE CENTER

And if you turn and look out beyond Piraeus, the port of Athens, you can imagine yourself back in ancient Greece. There lies the sea, blue in summertime, lashed with storms in winter, and scattered over with islands, large and small.

A temple of the sea-god Poseidon stands on the bold headland of Sunium, southeast of Athens, looking toward the islands of the Aegean Sea and the far-distant coast of Asia Minor beyond the horizon. This is the way to the island of Delos, with its shrine of Apollo; to Rhodes, so green and full of flowers; or, turning southward, to the great island of Crete.

25

The Greeks of the islands, separated by the treacherous sea, were as independent as the townsmen of the mainland cities, and even to this day many Greek islanders feel themselves in a foreign country when they come to mainland Greece.

The fishermen and seafarers of ancient times must often have prayed to Poseidon for fair weather and a safe journey as they sailed past his temple at Sunium. The Greeks had always been seafarers and adventurers. Their rocky land was too small to hold them, and much as they loved their homes, they launched out to seek their fortunes overseas.

26

ARTISTS AND ADVENTURERS

The old Greek tales of fantastic voyages may well be based
on real adventures. The sailing of the hero Jason and his
Argonauts, in search of the Golden Fleece, could have been a
journey to the Black Sea, and Homer could have gathered some
of his ideas for *The Odyssey* from the yarns of shipwrecked
sailors. The wanderings of Odysseus, among islands of enchant-
ment and monsters of the sea, may have followed the course of
some venture westward to Italy, Sicily and North Africa.

We know the Greeks went to all these places. They pushed
still farther afield, to southern France and Spain, and eastward
to Asia Minor and even to India.

They went not only as traders—and sometimes pirates—
but also as colonists to settle in the distant lands. As the towns
of Greece grew greater and richer, they sent out shiploads of
colonists to found new cities overseas. Some of the Greek cities

27

along the coast of Asia Minor, and in Italy and Sicily and around the shores of the Black Sea, became as wealthy and prosperous as the old towns at home, and the world of the Greeks was extended far beyond their own land.

Everywhere they settled, the Greeks took with them their artists, craftsmen and architects. Artists were necessary members of any community, and the things they made were a part of daily life, not just to be seen and enjoyed by a few.

The houses of the Greeks, even of rich men, were mostly simple and comfortless, and their food and clothes plain. Yet the ordinary jugs and bowls in the housewife's kitchen were finely shaped by the potter, and men drank their wine from elegant earthenware cups, decorated with beautiful paintings.

The metalworkers were the most highly respected of all craftsmen for the fineness of their work. They were the makers of bronze bowls and caldrons and tripods. They knew how to cast bronze figures, large and small, of animals, men and gods, and they could turn their hands to making coins and the most delicate golden jewelry.

Sculptors, stone-carvers and painters were needed to decorate temples and public buildings and to make statues of gods and famous citizens. There were weavers and woodcarvers too, but their work, along with most of the frail carvings in ivory, has perished in the centuries between their time and ours. Many wonderful things have been lost that were made in ancient Greece and the Greek cities overseas, but the miracle is that so much has survived for us to look at and enjoy.

The things we shall see in this book will lead us through six hundred years of Greek art, from the eighth to the second century B.C. It is difficult at first to think back so far, to bring to

life a people and a time so distant. Yet through their art the ancient Greeks begin to come alive again. Everything they made—from the Parthenon to a painted pot on a museum shelf—can open up for us a view of the men who made it, the people it was made for and the sort of life they knew.

In the eighth century, at the beginning of our story, the life of the Greeks was hard and dangerous. Their land was recovering from the years of fighting and misery known as the Dark Ages. A warlike people, the Dorians, had invaded Greece from the north in about the year 1200 B.C. The splendid palaces of the Bronze Age kings, the rulers of the land, were plundered and burned by the Dorians, and paintings, pottery and golden treasures were looted and destroyed.

But art did not die in Greece, even in the Dark Ages. Some of the painters, potters and metalworkers who had served the Bronze Age kings must have escaped from the burning palaces, and a few took refuge in Athens, a small and unimportant place in those days but with a strongly fortified acropolis. While other towns fell to the Dorian invaders, Athens somehow remained unconquered and gave shelter to homeless refugees.

With the coming of more peaceful times, when people had the strength and spirit to care about beautiful things, it was in Athens that Greek artists made a new start, the beginning of a great adventure. . . .

30

II THE SPRINGTIME OF
GREEK ART

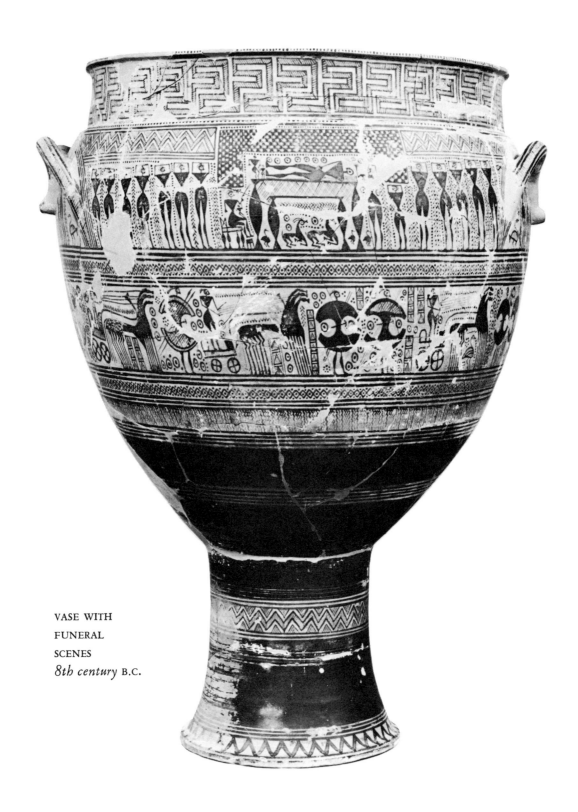

VASE WITH
FUNERAL
SCENES
8th century B.C.

ART AND GEOMETRY

BRONZE DEER
AND FAWN
(WITH A BIRD
PERCHED ON THE
DEER'S BACK)
8th century B.C.

Three hundred years before the Parthenon was built, a potter of Athens took good red clay and made this majestic vase. Standing nearly four feet tall, it was designed to be a memorial and to mark the grave of an eminent citizen in the cemetery outside the city gate.

When the potter had finished shaping the vase, a painter covered it with bands of intricate designs. Geometric patterns and little figures of birds and beasts were the usual decorations for pottery in those days, and in adding two scenes with human figures, this painter was doing something new and exciting. His people are hardly more than stick figures, but they are the beginning of great things to come.

In the upper scene he painted the dead man lying on a bier with lines of mourners on either side. Below is a funeral procession of warriors, bearing spears and the strangely shaped shields of the Greeks, and between the warriors are chariots of war, each drawn by three slender horses.

33

BRONZE HORSE
8th century B.C.

A little bronze horse, made about the same time as the vase, is as simple and geometric in shape as the painted horses. Although the sculptor did not attempt to copy a real animal, he grasped just what matters about a horse—the powerful curve of the neck, the ears alert, pricked forward, and the swelling muscles of thighs and shoulders. The figure seems alive and tense with energy.

Small sculptures like this one were given as gifts to the gods in their temples, just as live animals were presented for sacrifice. Many little figures of animals and people have been found at the shrine of Zeus at Olympia; others were buried in graves as offerings to the dead. A man who loved horses might have little clay horses buried beside him, and sometimes painted clay figures of mourners were placed in the grave by weeping friends.

34

CLAY FIGURE OF A MOURNER

A bronze warrior stands as stiffly as the people on the vase, but the tiny seated figure has life and movement. He is a maker of armor, an important craftsman in those warlike times, and the sculptor who cast the figure in bronze must have known something of the armorer's craft. He has shown the man hammering out a helmet, shaping it carefully over a metal stake.

TWO BRONZE
STATUETTES
8th century B.C.
Left WARRIOR
Below MAN MAKING
A HELMET

When the metalworkers turned to making jewelry, even a humble thing like a safety pin—very necessary when clothes had no buttons—became a work of art. This one is wrought in gold, with an antlered stag engraved on the square plate into which the catch was fitted.

FIBULA, OR
SAFETY PIN
8th century B.C.

Horses, stags and the little wild goats, which you can find on the big vase, were all familiar animals and common subjects for artists; but the curious jug opposite marks a new departure in animal designs.

On the front of it is a lion killing a stag, and the top of the jug is molded in the shape of a griffin's head with open beak. Animal-headed jugs were an Oriental idea. The lion and the fabulous griffin were both creatures of the East, and their appearance in Greek art is part of a story of adventure and exploration.

Greek merchants and colonists were pushing eastward to Asia Minor and Syria, Egypt and the shores of the Black Sea. They brought home to Greece and the islands rich metalwork, textiles and carved ivory decorated with designs of strange animals and plants, and soon not only lions and griffins but a whole menagerie of Eastern creatures found their way into Greek art.

36

GRIFFIN-HEADED
JUG 700–650 B.C.

MONSTERS

FROM THE ORIENT

The fabulous griffin, an imaginary mixture of lion and eagle, was a favorite animal with Greek artists. In the seventh century B.C. the rims of bronze caldrons were often decorated with the heads of guardian griffins, prick-eared and alert.

Caldrons were originally used as cooking pots, placed over the open fire on their tripods, but these elaborate ones were not intended for stewing meat or boiling porridge. They were works of art, worthy to be exchanged as gifts between rulers and nobles or awarded as prizes to athletes at the games, and they were especially acceptable as offerings to the gods.

Above BRONZE
GRIFFIN HEAD
About 630 B.C.

Small, sprightly griffins are perched on the shoulders of the young girl who forms the handle of a round mirror. The bronze disc was originally so brightly polished that a lady could admire her reflection in it. Perhaps the owner of the mirror wore a necklace of small golden plaques like this one, which comes from Rhodes. It is decorated with an Egyptian sphinx.

RHODIAN
WINE JUG
7th century B.C.

The lovely island of Rhodes lies close against the coast of Asia Minor, and was a natural stopping place for merchants from the Near East. This big wine jug is typical of the pottery found in Rhodes, with its painted design of Egyptian lotus flowers and lively wild goats. On the Rhodian pots, besides

40

lions and griffins, we find geese and swallows and wild boars and quantities of goats.

A very ancient folk song of Rhodes tells of the swallows' return with the fine spring weather, and here a Rhodian potter has made a little perfume bottle in the slender shape of a swallow, looking as though it were about to take wing.

The making of decorative little bottles for perfumes gave the potters a chance to experiment with new shapes and designs. The head of a lion forms the top of this tiny bottle from Corinth, and on the sides are miniature paintings of warriors in battle, a horse race and the hunting of a hare!

Above SCENT BOTTLE
MADE IN RHODES
About 600 B.C.
Right SCENT BOTTLE
MADE IN CORINTH
7th century B.C.

CORINTHIAN
WINE JUG
About 640–525 B.C.

The city of Corinth was famous for its pottery in the seventh century B.C., for the Corinthian painters had invented a new and brilliant method of decorating pots. The figures were painted in silhouette in a thin mixture of clay that would turn glossy black when fired in the kiln. Touches of white or purplish-red might be added, but the details of the figures, such as the muscles of the lions on the wine jug, were scratched in with a sharp tool and showed up as light lines. These Corinthian "black-figure" pots, especially the little scent bottles, were exported far and wide to the lands around the Mediterranean and even to the shores of the Black Sea.

COINS OF ASIA MINOR
WITH LION'S HEAD AND IBEX
7th century B.C.

42

CORINTHIAN WINE JUG
FOUND IN RHODES
625–600 B.C.

Corinth was so prosperous that it was among the first Greek cities to have coins of its own. Coinage was another idea that came to Greece from the East. The earliest coins were made in Asia Minor, where wealthy merchants and kings badly needed a better system of trading than the old way of barter and exchange.

Each coin was stamped with the special symbol of the city that had issued it. On a coin of Corinth we see the winged horse, Pegasus, famous in Greek mythology but originally a creature of the East; and on the back of the coin is a swastika.

43

COIN OF CORINTH
About 600 B.C.

ATHENIAN VASE
675–650 B.C.

NESSOS FALLS
BEFORE
HERAKLES
(*From the
painting on
the vase*)

The first Athenian coins were stamped with a picture of a waterpot, showing that the most important product of Athens was still painted pottery.

The Athenian potters, busy in their workshops near the cemetery and the city gate, were making very different pottery from the formal funeral vases with their geometric patterns. They had started to work in the black-figure style of Corinth, but instead of copying the neat Corinthian animal designs, the Athenians painted storytelling pictures on their pots, and made the figures large and bold.

On the neck of this big water jar a lion is attacking an ass; on the shoulder between the handles are grazing horses, and in the scene below, an exploit of the hero, Herakles. He has just slain the centaur Nessos, and he stands triumphant, sword in hand, with his four-horse chariot behind him.

The Athenians were interested, above all, in the doings of men and gods, and what they took from the Near East was something far more important than fantastic animal patterns. In Egypt the Greeks discovered a whole new form of art, and the Athenians joyfully made it their own.

45

ATHENIAN
COIN 594 B.C.

THE BEGINNINGS

OF MARBLE

SCULPTURE

In Egypt the Greeks first saw large stone sculptures, and were inspired to use the fine marble of their own land to make statues of men and gods.

This figure of a young man, carved in marble by a sculptor of Athens, may remind us of an Egyptian statue, but we can soon see the differences between them. The Egyptian statue is a portrait, while the Greek one could represent either a man or a god, Apollo or a young athlete. Then, too, the Egyptian statues were always clothed, as the people had been in life. The Greek figures were naked, to show the beauty of the human body, and their muscles were carved in simple forms and smoothed to the smoothness of ivory.

Marble is a hard stone, and the Greeks must have found it difficult to carve at first. The sculptor of this figure probably began shaping his long slab of marble while it lay in the quarry where it had been cut. He drilled small holes all over the surface

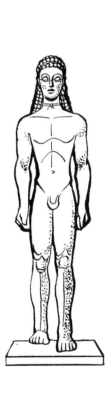

MARBLE STATUE
OF A YOUTH
Athenian,
end of 7th century B.C.

of the stone and then flaked off the little pieces of marble left between them. The half-finished statue would be pockmarked with round scars that had to be patiently rubbed away with emery and pumice stone.

The sculptor dared not cut too deeply into the marble for fear of breaking it. He left the hands of the figure joined to the thighs, and reinforced the neck by leaving the long hair hanging down to the shoulders.

He made the face of the young man calm and serious, like the faces of the Egyptian statues, but when the Greek sculptors became more sure of themselves as carvers in marble, their own joy came through and the faces of their figures broke into smiles. These first statues have a freshness and lightheartedness about them. To look at them makes you want to smile.

There is joy in the figure of a young man bringing a calf for sacrifice at the temple of Athena. Although the man's legs are broken away, you can feel the movement of his striding

48

forward with the little animal on his shoulders, its legs firmly
held in his strong hands. According to a carved inscription, this
statue was set up on the Acropolis in Athens by a man named
Rhombus. Like many marble statues at this time, it was made
as an offering to the goddess.

MARBLE STATUE OF
A MAN WITH A CALF
About 575 B.C.

49

50

For people who could afford them, the favorite offerings to Athena's temple were marble figures of young girls, dressed in the fashion of the time. This one wears a *peplos,* the simple draped costume of mainland Greece. There are traces of a green-painted pattern on her dress, and her hair and lips are colored brownish-red. The Greeks always colored their marble statues, and even the naked figures were lightly stained and waxed, to make them look more lifelike.

THE PEPLOS

This smiling statue, so simple in design, is full of life; and although she stands still, with feet together, we feel as though at any moment she could begin to dance.

The crouching sphinx has the same feeling of movement. Her head is alert; the hindquarters are gathered together ready to spring, and the upsweep of the wings adds to the sense of lightness. There is nothing sad or funereal about this figure, yet

MARBLE SPHINX
6th century B.C.

51

THE YOUNG MAN
MEGAKLES AND
HIS SISTER GORGO

MARBLE GRAVESTONE
6th century B.C.

she sits on the top of a gravestone, which was set up in memory of a young man and his small sister. The two figures, side by side, are carved on the stone in low relief, and there are still scraps of reddish color on their hair and on the background. Each holds a flower, and the young man has a little oil jar hanging from his wrist, such as athletes used to carry, ready to rub himself with oil after exercise.

52

The smiling head on page 48 also comes from the gravestone of an athlete. He must have been a champion discus thrower, for you can see the round discus behind his head.

The vivid scenes of athletes in training were carved on the base of a statue. We see young men wrestling and playing ball games. One leans over to test the point of his javelin, and another is poised to start running a race.

Sports and games were an essential part of a boy's education in ancient Greece. Victorious athletes were the heroes of their cities, and many boys must have dreamed of winning prizes and

TWO MARBLE
RELIEF CARVINGS
OF ATHLETES
6th century B.C.

FRIEZE FROM
THE TREASURY
OF THE SIPHNIANS
AT DELPHI 525 B.C.

lifelong fame at the great games at Olympia and Delphi. The Greeks believed in training both the body and the mind, to make a well-rounded person. Athletics also prepared men for war and for the defense of their city in time of invasion.

This battle scene is part of a sculptured frieze. The battle is a legendary one between gods and giants, but the giants are armed like Greek foot soldiers, with helmets, round shields and spears. In spite of their strength, the giants are doomed to defeat. One of them flees before Apollo and Artemis, who stride into battle side by side, and another giant falls victim

54

to the lions that draw the chariot of the goddess Cybele.

The frieze is the earliest stone sculpture we have seen that was made to decorate a building; from now on we shall find builders and sculptors working closely together. By the time this frieze was carved, the Greeks were building stone temples for the gods. This was another lesson they had learned from the Egyptians; but just as they breathed new life into the old Egyptian idea of figure sculpture, so they developed their own style of building to give delight to men and gods.

55

TEMPLE OF APOLLO
AT CORINTH
6th century B.C.

STONE HOUSES FOR THE GODS

The massive columns of the Temple of Apollo at Corinth, each carved from a single slab of stone, were set up in the sixth century B.C., when the idea of building stone temples was still new in Greece.

Greek temples until then were simple buildings of wood and brick. After the Greeks had seen and admired the great temples of Egypt and had begun to build in stone themselves, it was natural that the rich and enterprising city of Corinth should take the lead. The Temple of Apollo is the oldest one in Greece with some of its original columns still standing, battered by centuries of storms and earthquakes and the strife of men.

But how did a temple look when it was new?

57

The Greeks worshiped out of doors, and their temples were not like churches or synagogues, designed to hold a congregation of people. The building was meant to house only a large statue of the god, together with some of the temple treasures; and the simplest kind of temple was just a hall, called a *cella,* with a gabled roof and a porch in front, supported by columns.

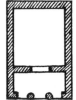

PLANS OF GREEK TEMPLES

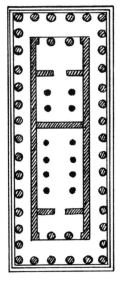

Temple of Apollo, Corinth

BRONZE GOAT
6th century B.C.

In bigger temples the porch was extended to make a colonnade all around, and the cella might be so wide that two rows of columns were built inside to support the roof; but the worshipers still gathered out of doors.

Under the open sky the pungent smoke arose from the altar of the god, where burnt sacrifices of the fat and bones of animals were offered up. Small bronze statues of animals and people, as we have seen, were also presented as offerings, while larger statues

58

Pediment

Acroterion

Triglyph
Metope

Capital

Fluted shaft

Architrave

DORIC TEMPLE AND
ITS DECORATION

dedicated to the god, such as marble figures of men and girls, were crowded into the space around the temple.

The building itself, like a piece of sculpture, was meant to be seen and enjoyed from outside. The drawing shows the richness of carved and painted decoration on a temple in the Doric style. A Doric temple, like the one at Corinth, always had simple massive columns with plain capitals to support the horizontal architrave; but above them, in the square panels called *metopes,* there was usually a series of carved reliefs illustrating heroic tales such as the stories of Herakles. The pediments, the triangular spaces at the gable ends of the temple, provided a place for much larger sculptures, which often told legends of the god to whom the temple was dedicated.

59

BRONZE STATUETTE
OF A SHEPHERD
WITH HIS OFFERINGS
6th century B.C.

While the Doric style was the favorite in mainland Greece and in the great Greek cities in Italy and Sicily, the Ionic style, developed by the Greeks in Asia Minor, spread to the mainland in the sixth century B.C. The columns of an Ionic temple were more slender than the Doric ones and had elaborately carved capitals; and sometimes they were replaced by standing figures that supported the architrave on their heads.

Above the columns there were no metopes, but a long frieze, carved in relief and gaily painted. The frieze on page 54—the battle between gods and giants—originally adorned a treasury at the Shrine of Apollo at Delphi. It was a beautiful small building in the Ionic style that held the rich gifts presented to the shrine by the people of the island of Siphnos.

PROCESSION WITH ANIMALS FOR SACRIFICE *From a painted vase, 6th century* B.C.

At important shrines and sacred places there were many lesser buildings grouped around the main temple of the god, and especially at Delphi, where the shrine was the home of the famous Oracle.

For the Greeks, Delphi was the center of the world. Pilgrims found their way there from all parts of Greece and from all the lands where Greeks had settled; and if we follow them today we can still see something of what they saw, and feel a little of their awe and wonder.

IONIC TEMPLE:
THE ERECHTHEUM
IN ATHENS
(*See page 106*)

61

THE SHRINE OF APOLLO AT DELPHI

THE SHRINE OF APOLLO

High on the slopes of Mount Parnassus the ruins of Apollo's shrine seem to grow out of the mountainside. Between the foundations of the buildings the Sacred Way of the pilgrims curves upward to the great platform and the few standing columns of Apollo's temple.

Delphi was a sacred place long before the building of a temple there. The earth at Delphi was strangely disturbed. The earthquakes that destroyed the first stone temple were a constant threat to the shrine, sending huge boulders hurtling down from the cliffs above, where eagles, the birds of Zeus, soared in the blue air.

Out of fissures in the rock came mysterious gases from deep in the earth. They poured forth in a little chamber underneath the Temple of Apollo, and it was here that the priestess, seated on a tripod, passed into a trance and cried out the words of the Delphic Oracle, wild, incoherent words that had to be interpreted to the hearers by the priests of the temple.

The Oracle was consulted not only by kings and statesmen and generals but also by all kinds of lesser people in need of

TRIPOD AND
FIGURE OF APOLLO
*Two Greek coins,
6th century* B.C.

63

advice. Pilgrims were constantly coming to Delphi along the mountain road from Athens or by ship across the Gulf of Corinth; but the greatest crowds came every four years at the time of the Pythic Games.

Then there was a grand procession up the Sacred Way to Apollo's temple, beginning at the Castalian Spring, the holy water that still flows from a deep cut between the cliffs. Past the treasuries of cities that had given rich gifts to the shrine, the procession would wind its way with music and song, and in front of the temple animals would be slaughtered and sacrificed to the god to mark the opening of the games.

Above the temple, still higher up the mountain, was a

ATHLETE THROWING
THE DISCUS
*From a painted cup,
about 480* B.C.

APOLLO WITH
HIS LYRE
*From a painted vase,
5th century* B.C.

theater for the performance of plays, for drama was pleasing to
Apollo, the god of music and poetry. Highest of all lay the
stadium, where people thronged the mountain slope to watch
the athletes competing to the glory of the god.

65

The famous Charioteer of Delphi commemorates a victory
in the Pythic Games.

The young man must originally have stood in his chariot,
holding the reins of the horses. The whole group was cast in
bronze, and probably the sculptor first carved the figures in wood
and used these as models in making his clay molds for the metal.

How different this figure is from those we have seen! The
lightheartedness and smile have gone, and there is no feeling
of movement; even the folds of the long gown fall like the
fluted carvings on a column. The fury and danger of the chariot
race are past, and the chariot is still. The young man stands
proudly and solemnly, reminding us that the games were a part
of worship and that the god Apollo demanded calmness and
restraint from his worshipers, and "Nothing to excess."

The charioteer must have stood outside the Temple of Apollo,
as an offering, and it gives us an idea of some of the wonderful
works of art that have been lost. Artists, builders and painters
used their greatest skill to adorn the shrines of the gods with
beautiful buildings and sculptures.

There was great art at Delphi but even more at Olympia,
the Shrine of Zeus and the home of the most famous games
in all of ancient Greece.

THE GAMES AT OLYMPIA

Olympia is a quiet place today. It is hard to imagine all the excitement of the games, when people gathered there from far and near and camped out in the lush green valley that surrounded the sacred buildings and the stadium.

Every four years in late summer, when the games were held, a truce was declared throughout the land. Weapons were laid aside and fighting ceased between rival cities, so that athletes and spectators might travel to Olympia and return to their homes in peace.

The athletes spent a month in training at Elis, twenty-four miles away, moving in procession to Olympia three days before the games began. On the way there they paused for a sacrifice to Zeus, and the priests reminded them that all athletes must be pure in body and mind, in thought and deed, to be worthy to compete in the games.

The first day of the five-day festival was given up to practice and preparation; the climax came at noon when a hog and a

Above ATHLETE AND TRAINER *From a painted cup,* 480 B.C.

sheep were offered up to Zeus, and each athlete vowed to compete in true sportsmanship and honesty. In the shadow of the
mighty temple of Zeus at Olympia no one could forget that
competitors in the games bore a sacred responsibility and performed an act of faith and worship.

THE RUINS AT OLYMPIA

69

SCULPTURES FROM
THE EAST PEDIMENT
OF THE TEMPLE OF ZEUS
About 460 B.C.

The Temple of Zeus, built in the fifth century B.C., was justly famous in the ancient world. It far surpassed in size and splendor the older temple at Olympia, dedicated to Hera, queen of the gods.

The outside of the Temple of Zeus was richly adorned with marble sculpture, and within stood a wonderful statue of the god, made of gold and ivory, a masterpiece of the sculptor, Phidias. Coming to Olympia from Athens, the sculptor had made the statue on the spot, in a temporary workshop close by the temple. Fragments of ivory and some molds for shaping the gold have been found there, along with the sculptor's own drinking cup, with "I belong to Phidias" scratched on the bottom.

His renowned statue of Zeus, which brought joy and comfort to all who gazed on it, has long since been destroyed, but

70

some of the other sculptures from the temple have survived. We can still see some of the metopes with vigorous reliefs showing exploits of Herakles, and parts of the two magnificent pediments.

On the pediment at the east end of the temple was a quiet scene of preparations for a chariot race between the young man Pelops and King Oinomaos of Elis.

If Pelops could beat the king, he would win the hand of the king's daughter, as many before him had tried to do. Unlike the athletes in the games, Pelops was to win the race by cheating. He bribed the king's charioteer to replace the linchpins of the royal chariot with pieces of wax, so that the chariot collapsed at the height of the race and Oinomaos was hurled to the ground and killed.

HERAKLES AND THE CRETAN BULL
(METOPE FROM THE TEMPLE OF ZEUS)

The western pediment was filled with a furious battle between centaurs and their legendary enemies, the tribe of lapiths.
In the midst of the fighting, the only peaceful figure was the
god Apollo, standing tall and straight, with one arm outstretched. His stillness reminds us of the bronze charioteer at
Delphi, and the strong figure of the god might well have been
inspired by the contestants in the Olympic Games.

In the dust and summer heat of Olympia, the athletes com-
peted in the stadium, running, wrestling, boxing, broad jump-

72

APOLLO
(WEST PEDIMENT OF THE TEMPLE OF ZEUS)

BOXERS
*From a painted
vase, 6th century* B.C.

ing and throwing discus and javelin. Chariot and horse races were run in the hippodrome before wildly cheering crowds.

Nearly all the contests were crowded into the second day of the festival. The third day was the time for rest and celebration and for the sacrifice of a hundred bulls on the altar outside the Temple of Zeus. Contests for young boys were held on that day and the next, and the festival ended on the fifth day with rejoicing, final sacrifices and the reading of the list of victors before the altar of Zeus.

The victors received no costly prizes, only wreaths of the wild olive that still grows among the ruins at Olympia; but they were assured of a hero's welcome and lifelong fame when they returned to their own cities. In Athens an Olympic victor had the right to eat free meals at the town hall and to sit in a prominent place at public games. Athens had its own athletic festival in honor of Athena, and here the Athenian painters and potters had an important part to play.

SILVER COIN
OF ATHENS
566 B.C.

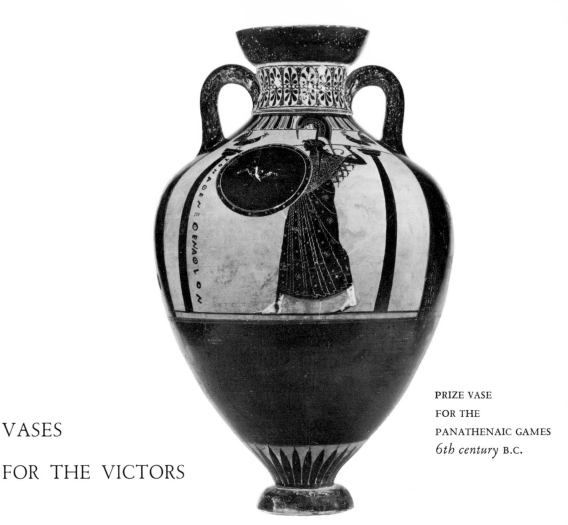

PRIZE VASE
FOR THE
PANATHENAIC GAMES
6th century B.C.

VASES

FOR THE VICTORS

The year 566 B.C., when the games in honor of Athena began, was such an important date in the history of Athens that a new coin was minted to commemorate it. The coin bore the helmeted head of Athena, and on the reverse was her bird, the little owl.

The Panathenaic Games, as they were called, were held in Athens every four years at the festival of the goddess, and as prizes the victors received large and handsome jars of oil, the finest painted pottery the Athenians could produce.

75

Each jar was decorated in the black-figure style with a painting of Athena on one side, and, on the other, a vivid picture of an athletic event.

Here we see a two-hundred-yard footrace, with the runners exerting every ounce of energy, arms and legs swinging and knees raised high in a powerful stride. In the horse race opposite, the jockeys ride bareback, the reins loose in their hands, and the horses leap forward, needing no whip or spur.

The bold figures fit beautifully on the curved surface of the vase, and the drawing is delicate and fine. Painters and potters had mastered their difficult craft to perfection, and their works are among the loveliest and most exciting things in all Greek art.

Above RUNNERS
Painting on a prize vase, 6th century B.C.

76

HORSE RACE
*Painting on the other
side of the vase
on page 75*

POTTERS

AND PAINTERS

The painted pottery of Athens forms such a picture gallery of animals, men and gods that it is easy to forget that these jars and jugs and cups were severely practical in design. They were made for use and were a necessary part of the household. Even the prize vases of the athletes were intended for the storage of oil, and each shape of pot had its own special purpose.

The woman of the house would fetch water at the public fountain in a large three-handled water jar called a *hydria,* as we can see in a picture painted on one of these jars.

78

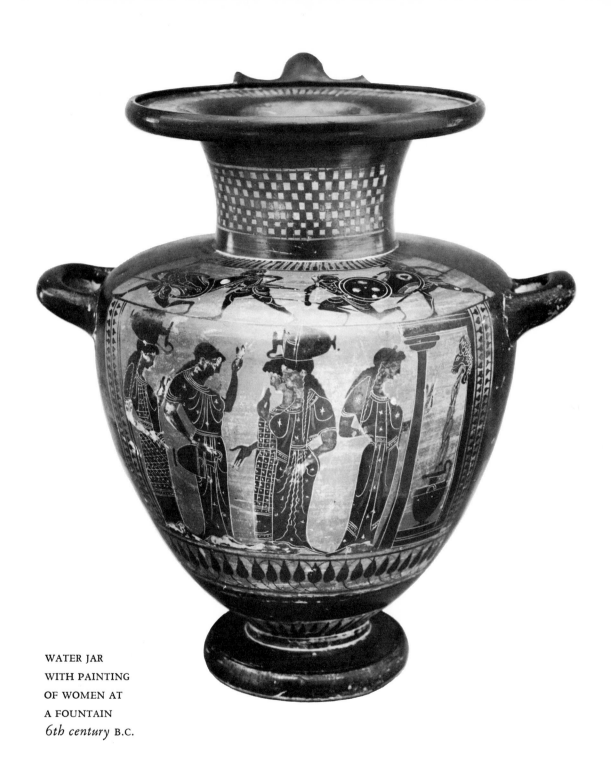

WATER JAR
WITH PAINTING
OF WOMEN AT
A FOUNTAIN
6th century B.C.

Water or wine was stored in a two-handled *amphora* like this one, with its masterly design of Herakles capturing the Cretan bull.

AMPHORA
WITH PAINTING
OF HERAKLES ROPING
THE CRETAN BULL
6th century B.C.

Herakles, as we have seen, was a favorite subject for painters and sculptors. We find him again on a small, slender oil jar,

HERAKLES AND
A CENTAUR *From
a painted oil jar,
6th century* B.C.

a *lekythos*. He is clothed in his usual lion skin, and is being entertained by a bearded centaur.

The lekythos on page 78 has a painting of athletes practicing to the music of a double flute. The youth at the left carries javelins, while the one at the right is completing a broad jump, swinging back the stone weights in his hands to throw his body forward as he hits the ground.

The beautiful two-handled *kylix* below was a cup for drinking wine. Many were decorated, like this one, with a single delicately drawn figure of an animal.

DRINKING CUP
WITH PAINTING
OF A STAG
6th century B.C.

MIXING BOWL WITH PAINTING OF FIGHT BETWEEN APOLLO AND HERAKLES
6th century B.C.

THESEUS SLAYING
THE MINOTAUR
*From a painted
cup like the one
on page 81*

The wine of the Greeks was very sweet, and they drank it generously diluted with water. The large bowls called *kraters,* used for mixing water and wine at the table, gave the painter a fine spacious field for his art.

This one is decorated inside and out. Around the top are animals, real and fantastic, and inside the lip is a picture of a choppy sea with leaping dolphins and a warship like those in the famous Athenian fleet. On the body of the krater is Herakles once more, club in hand, struggling to seize from Apollo the tripod of Delphi. They are flanked by chariots with charioteers who crane their necks to watch the fight, while Athena, the supporter of Herakles, and Artemis, the sister of Apollo, look on with equal interest.

The names of the figures on the krater are written in neat Greek letters on the background. Sometimes the potters and painters signed their own names on their works. Even when there is no signature it is often possible to tell one painter from another by their different styles of painting.

83

KANTHAROS

SKYPHOS

KYLIX

SHAPES OF
DRINKING CUPS

One of the finest painters of black-figure pots was a man named Exekias, whose pictures have a majestic stillness, reminding us again of the Delphic charioteer.

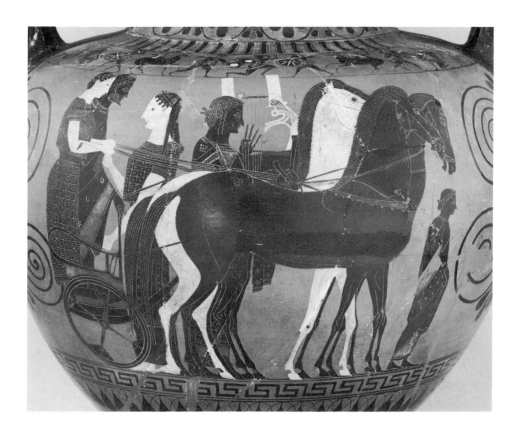

Another excellent painter, whose name is unknown, was a man who often worked for a potter named Andokides. This artist was not content to follow the old style of black-figure painting. If we compare his picture of Herakles and the tripod with the one on the krater, we not only find his design simpler and more striking but the whole effect quite different.

84

Instead of painting figures in black silhouette on the red clay, this painter covered the background with black and left the figures to stand out in red, adding the details of the bodies

FIGHT FOR THE TRIPOD *From an amphora painted by the Andokides Painter, 6th century* B.C.

in thin black lines. This was the beginning of "red-figure" pottery. Soon other painters took up the new style, and the old black-figure technique gradually passed out of use.

The new method was not easier than the old one. The figures had to be drawn in outline with a sure and steady hand before the black background was filled in around them. The

85

mixture used for painting was too thick to flow from a brush without being watered down, and the best painters learned to squeeze it out through a thin tube so that the black lines were raised a little from the surface of the pot. Yet they could still draw with grace and freedom.

The painters were at their best in decorating the drinking cups used at banquets. While the pictures on the outside were only appreciated when the cup was hanging on the wall, the

PAINTER
DECORATING
A CUP
*Fragment of
a painted cup,
5th century* B.C.

86

WARRIOR
AND BOY
Painting inside a cup,
about 490 B.C.

round picture within could be admired by the drinker as he drained his wine. Most of these paintings were scenes of drinking and dancing, livelier and more cheerful than this graceful drawing of a warrior and a boy.

Early in the fifth century, when this cup was made, warriors were a familiar sight in Athens, and every able-bodied man was

87

BRONZE WARRIOR FROM SPARTA
About 490 B.C.

needed for the protection of the city. The Greeks were desperately defending themselves against the onslaught of the Persians. The whole might of the Persian Empire had been flung against them.

In 480 B.C. the Persians captured Athens and pillaged the buildings on the Acropolis, which had been for so long a stronghold and a sacred place. The people of Athens had fled their homes and abandoned the city to the invader, but they still had their famous fleet.

They inflicted a crushing defeat on the Persians at the sea battle of Salamis, and returned to their battered city as proud victors. The ruins on the Acropolis only inspired the Athenians to raise new and nobler buildings there, worthy of the city's greatness, and, above all, to build a temple of Athena more beautiful than any temple in the world.

HORSEMEN
FROM THE FRIEZE
OF THE PARTHENON

88

III ATHENS AND THE
CLASSICAL AGE

THE PARTHENON AND

THE GREAT PROCESSION

After the defeat of the Persians, Athens was more than ever a leader among the city-states of Greece, in wealth and power and in the glory of her art. She became the head of a strong league of cities for defense against invasion, and the league quickly grew into an Athenian empire, with its funds of gold and silver stored in Athens. What better use could there be for this treasure than to help make the city beautiful and glorify the patron goddess who had given victory in battle?

90

HORSEMEN FROM THE FRIEZE OF THE PARTHENON

So thought the Athenians, under the leadership of their great statesman Pericles.

They had cleared away the ruins on the Acropolis, reverently burying the broken statues of young men and girls, set up long ago outside the old temple of Athena. The site for the new temple was ready; and at last, in the middle of the fifth century B.C., the building of the Parthenon began.

CENTAUR AND
FALLEN LAPITH
(METOPE FROM THE
PARTHENON)

The architects of the Parthenon, Ictinus and Callicrates, chose to build the temple in the Doric style. The great hall, or cella, lying roughly east and west, was divided into two rooms and had entrances at both ends. Over each doorway was a pillared porch of six columns, and all around the building, a massive colonnade.

The main entrance was to the east, and in the big eastern chamber a statue of Athena in gold and ivory towered to the ceiling. The sculptor was Phidias, who had made the famous statue of Zeus at Olympia, and it was he who probably planned and designed the rich sculptures around the outside of the temple.

On the pediments at either end of the Parthenon were scenes from mythology with the great figures carved in the round, as they had been at Olympia. Above the colonnade that encircled the temple were the square metopes, carved in high relief with

92

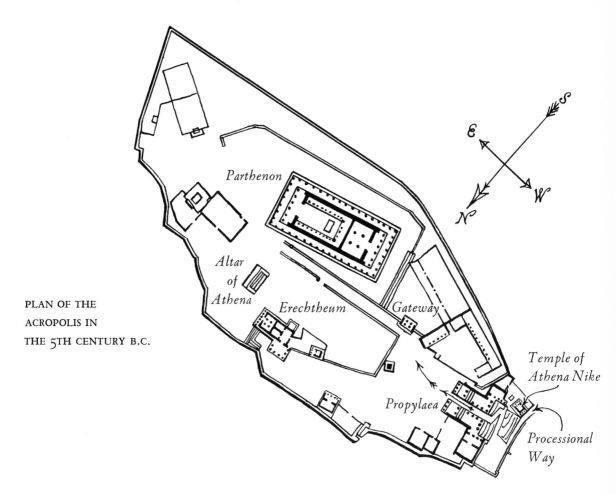

Parthenon

Altar of Athena

Erechtheum

Gateway

Temple of Athena Nike

Propylaea

Processional Way

a series of battles. Gods fought with giants, lapiths with centaurs, and Greeks with Amazons—those fiery warrior-women who were supposed to have invaded Athens long ago and met defeat at the hands of the hero Theseus.

Finally, over the porches and all down the long sides of the cella stretched a continuous frieze, not an illustration of myth or legend but a picture of the Athenians themselves, scores of them, taking part in the great Panathenaic Procession on the feast day of Athena.

As the sculptors planned it, the whole story of the procession could be read in the frieze, beginning at the western end

93

of the temple and moving down the long sides to its climax over the eastern doorway. The figures were carved in low relief and brightly painted, but they must have been hard to see so high up behind the colonnade.

Today, when a large part of the frieze is among the Elgin marbles in the British Museum, we have a much closer view of it than the Greeks ever had when the sculptures were in place on the temple. As the figures pass before us, we are caught up in the procession, pressing forward to the Acropolis from the town below.

Every year the birthday of the goddess was celebrated by the joyful marching of hundreds of citizens to the Acropolis, but the frieze shows us the far more splendid procession that went forth every four years, when the Panathenaic Games were

94

HORSEMEN
AT FULL SPEED

held. At its head was a company of girls bearing a new garment, the peplos, for the ancient wooden statue of Athena that used to stand in the old temple.

In Athens today, we can still trace the course of the procession. Its starting point was the Dipylon Gate of the city near the old cemetery and the workshops of the potters. Here the people assembled with the sacrificial animals, the riders mounted their eager horses, and the girls took up the folded peplos and the baskets of offerings for the goddess.

START OF THE
PROCESSION:
HORSEMEN
PREPARING TO MOUNT

Chariots also formed part of the procession as it moved across the Agora, the main market place at the heart of the city. Here we can walk up the same broad, dusty road that the people followed. At the upper boundary of the Agora the horses must have slowed their pace, for the road grows steeper as it climbs the hillside toward the Acropolis.

Passing below the rocky hill of Areopagus, the people made for the great gateway of the Acropolis, the Propylaea. As they drew near to it, the road narrowed and began to zigzag over the rocks. Here the chariots, and perhaps the horsemen, must

THE PROPYLAEA, GATEWAY OF THE ACROPOLIS *Built about 437–432* B.C.

have turned back, for the way through the Propylaea was steep, narrow and slippery, as it still is today. The whole building—far more than a simple gateway—was skillfully fitted into the steep side of the hill, and even now, when it stands in ruins, we can understand why the Greeks praised it as highly as the Parthenon.

97

As we follow the procession through the inner passage of the gateway, flanked by Ionic columns, we can look out to the temple of the victorious Athena—Athena Nike—perched high on a jutting promontory of stone. It is a miniature Ionic temple, built some years later than the Parthenon, and with a frieze of fighting Greeks and Persians.

And now at last, in the wake of the procession, we climb
to the summit of the Acropolis and see the Parthenon.

THE PARTHENON
FROM THE NORTHWEST
Built 447–433 B.C.

For us, the temple bursts into view with nothing to hide it; for the people in the procession, the Parthenon was half hidden by other buildings, and the first thing they saw was a tall statue of Athena that stood opposite the Propylaea. Then the leaders of the procession moved slowly to the right, and everyone could gaze in awe at the western end of the Parthenon and the carved and painted figures of the pediment.

The scene they saw there was the famous contest between Athena and Poseidon to decide which should be patron of Athens. Each performed a miracle as a proof of power. Poseidon struck a rock with his trident, and out gushed a spring of salt water; but at Athena's command the first olive tree sprang up, and for this gift to Athens, Athena was declared the winner. The two contestants were tall, heroic figures in the middle of the pediment, with their chariots beside them, while smaller figures looked on, sitting and lying down in the narrow spaces at the ends.

EAST END OF
THE PARTHENON
At the west door of the Parthenon the procession may have split in two, to pass along both sides of the temple and come together at the main doorway in the eastern end.

There the pediment sculptures told the strange story of the birth of Athena from the brow of Zeus, which Hephaistos the smith had cut open with an ax. Some of the sculptures from this pediment were saved among the Elgin marbles, and still in

place in the extreme corners we can see the noble horses' heads
that indicated the time of day when Athena was born. It was
dawn, and the horses of the sun-god's chariot were rising on the
left, while to the right the weary horses of the moon were sink-
ing out of sight.

Over the eastern porch of the Parthenon the frieze showed
the end and climax of the great procession. Here the gods themselves were seated, facing outward to greet the citizens as they
approached along the north and south sides of the temple.

103

FRIEZE AT THE
EAST END OF
THE PARTHENON

The sculptors made the gods bigger than ordinary mortals, but there is nothing else to distinguish them from the people of Athens. The gods were originally flanked by two groups of dignified elderly men—Athenian heroes, four of whom can be seen standing next to Hermes and Dionysos.

ATHENA

DEMETER   ARES   HERA   ZEUS

The climax of the frieze—and procession—comes with the few quiet figures between the groups of gods. This scene actually took place, not in the Parthenon, but in the Erech- theum, the smaller temple that marked the site of Athena's contest with Poseidon. The Erechtheum was the goal of the

HEPHAISTOS   POSEIDON   APOLLO   ARTEMIS

great procession. Here the girls presented the new robe for the goddess to the officials of the temple, and at the altar of Athena nearby the beasts were slaughtered for sacrifice and the people rejoiced as the dark smoke rose into the summer sky.

SOUTH PORCH
OF THE
ERECHTHEUM

The altar of Athena is gone, but the Erechtheum still stands. It is a lovely temple in Ionic style, a contrast to the massive strength of the Parthenon. On its south side, facing the Parthenon, is a little porch where figures of young women take the place of columns to support the roof. Solemn and beautiful, how different they are from the joyous sculptures of a hundred years before—the men and girls with their springtime freshness and simplicity and their delighted smiles!

In the sculptures of the Parthenon too—both men and gods—we see this same high seriousness and calm beauty. The

great procession must have been full of dust and heat and excitement, the clatter of hoofs, the shouts of men and the frantic bellowing of beasts for sacrifice; but you could never guess this from the frieze, with its orderly rhythm of cantering horses in close-set ranks, and people moving sedately on foot, their faces always peaceful and serene. The artists had their own vision of the world, not as it really was but as they felt it should be.

The calmness and nobility they expressed were fitting for a temple and a solemn religious occasion, but all life was not

ONE OF THE
MAIDENS FROM
THE SOUTH PORCH
OF THE ERECHTHEUM

like that, as the artists themselves knew well. Below the Acropolis were the bustling streets of the city and the mean small houses crowded together. The people who lived there could enjoy the wonderful art of the Parthenon, but in their own homes they took delight in simpler, less noble, things. Their lives were full of hardship; they needed the tonic of laughter, and they had a sense of humor that nothing could keep down.

COMEDY IN CLAY

This worried old woman with a baby is one of the many little clay sculptures that the people of Athens enjoyed. She had special meaning for lovers of the theater, for she is a character from a Greek comedy, and belongs to a set of actor-figures, representing the whole cast of a play. Most of her companions are men who wear the broadly smiling masks of comic actors and have their costumes generously padded over the stomach. In reality, there were no women on the stage, and all their parts were played by men.

Nearly everyone in Athens loved the theater. Each year, in early spring, at the great festival in honor of Dionysos, the whole city was on holiday, and the people crowded into the

109

CLAY FIGURES

OF ACTORS

4th century B.C.

open-air theater on the steep hillside below the Acropolis. Shivering in the spring chill, they sat close-packed on the tiers of hard wooden benches that climbed the slope, and watched and listened spellbound, for days on end, while comedy and tragedy were played out on the circular stage at the foot of the hill. The people were carried away by the glorious poetry of the tragedies, but it was the rough, hearty laughter of the comedies that they wanted to be reminded of throughout the year. They chose the comic figures to decorate their houses and to bury in the graves of ardent theatergoers.

The little statues of actors were so popular that they were cast in molds for ease and speed in the making, instead of being

CLAY TOYS:
MAN ON A GOOSE
About 480 B.C.
MONKEY *About 420* B.C.
JOINTED DOLL
About 350 B.C.

modeled by hand. The children's toys of clay, like the gaily-painted man riding a goose and the monkey eating a stolen cake, were carefully modeled, one by one. Corinthian craftsmen were particularly skilled at toymaking, and even made jointed dolls for little girls to dress.

Some of the small clay models, although they were not actually made in Athens, seem to take us straight into the every-

VISIT TO THE
BARBER
5th century B.C.

day life of the city—to the barbershop where the bearded customer sits slumped in the chair, and into the kitchen where a woman bakes cakes in an earthenware oven.

Athenian housewives depended on the potters to make all the kitchen pots and pans, as well as elegant vessels for the table, and the potters and painters were always busy in their workshops by the city gate.

WOMAN BAKING
Late 6th century B.C.

POTTERY,

PAINTING

AND SCULPTURE

Athenian kitchens were stocked with all shapes and sizes of pots and pans, made of plain red earthenware or painted and fired to a glossy black. Besides the pottery ovens for baking cakes and bread, there were earthenware stewpots and casseroles, grills and frying pans. Houses were lighted by little pottery lamps, and people even bathed in pottery bathtubs, large enough for lying down in comfort.

Jugs for wine were always useful in the kitchen and at table, and tiny jugs were given as presents to children. They were painted in the red-figure style, which was used for most of the decorated pottery made in the fifth century, from little jugs like this one to the big kraters for mixing wine.

113

Above SMALL JUG
5th–4th century B.C.

MIXING BOWL
About 450 B.C.

This elegant krater with its scrolled handles must have made a handsome display piece for parties. On the neck between the handles the painter has pictured a domestic scene with a young man visiting a girl, while the large painting below is of a thrilling battle between Greeks and Amazons.

The krater is quite different from the one we saw before (on page 82). The shape has changed; the figures are red instead of black; and the painter's design is much less strict. In the battle scene, the people are not all drawn in side view, as they were in the older paintings, nor do they all stand firmly on the bottom border of the picture. Those behind the horses are set higher up, to show that they are farther away.

What had happened was that the vase painters were beginning to imitate a completely different kind of painting—the large wall paintings in which artists had room to show perspective and even landscape backgrounds. There was not space for all this on a vase, and the vase painters were trying to do something that was not really suitable for their art.

Wall paintings were done on a light background, and the vase painters began to copy this idea too. Instead of working boldly in black and red, they would cover the surface of a vase with a coat of thin white clay and then sketch the drawing in a few light lines, tinting it with soft red, brown and purple.

SHAPES OF
MIXING BOWLS

COLUMN KRATER

VOLUTE KRATER

115

FUNERAL VASE
5th century B.C.

The favorite pots for this kind of work were the slender oil jars, but they were not meant for ordinary use, as the white clay easily chipped off. Vases like the one opposite, with a picture of a young man beside a tall tombstone, were buried in graves as offerings. The drawings on the best of them were as simple and beautiful as the carvings on the old gravestones, and often they showed the dead people as they had been in life—a man putting on his armor or a woman looking at her jewels.

While the painters experimented with new kinds of decoration, the potters ventured into new shapes and designs, especially for drinking cups. They made cups shaped like the heads of rams or horses or people, and here is one in the form of a cow's hoof, with a painting of a boy herding cows around the top.

DRINKING CUP
About 470–460 B.C.

GUEST AT A BANQUET
From a painted cup,
about 500 B.C.

An Athenian potter, Sotades, was the maker of this cup in the shape of an Amazon on horseback. It was once brightly colored, with the Amazon dressed in a blue-and-red tunic and purple trousers and mounted on a white horse with red harness. On the base were pictures of a lion and a wild boar, and on the cup itself, rising above the rider's head, is a red-figure painting of fighting Amazons and Greeks. We can guess that this was more of an ornament or a conversation piece than a much-used drinking cup!

Here the potter has become a sculptor, and, like so many artists of his time, he has studied the sculptures of the Parthenon; his small clay figure has caught something of their grace and quiet joy.

118

DRINKING CUP *About 440* B.C.

SCULPTURES

IN BRONZE

BRONZE GOD
About 460 B.C.

The potters and metalworkers of Athens seem to have taken a keen interest in each other's work. One vase painter decorated a drinking cup with pictures of a bronze foundry, showing how statues were made. Large figures, such as the charioteer of Delphi and this splendid bronze god, were cast in separate pieces. In the

120

painting we see a craftsman hammering together the parts of a life-size statue, and then helping a second man to smooth down and finish the heroic figure of a warrior, still rough from the casting.

Few Greek bronzes of this size have survived; they were nearly all melted down in later years and the metal used again. The bronze god escaped destruction only by accident, through being sunk in a shipwreck and lying for centuries under the sea. A strong, bearded man caught in the action of throwing something—he may represent either Zeus or Poseidon, for his out-flung right hand could have held the thunderbolt of Zeus or the sea-god's trident.

SCENES IN A
BRONZE FOUNDRY
From a painted cup

BRONZE JUG
4th century B.C.

Many small bronze statues of gods and heroes and athletes have come down to us today, and some may be copies of larger figures, now lost.

The metalworkers also made handsome bronze water jugs and highly polished bronze mirrors. Some of the mirrors, like that on page 39, had statuettes as handles, but the later fashion was to make mirrors enclosed in round metal boxes. The lids were frequently decorated with designs in relief, such as the woman's head opposite, with curly, windblown hair. She is shown wear-

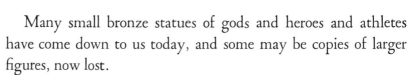

BRONZE STATUETTE OF A DISCUS THROWER
About 480 B.C.

WOMAN WITH
HER JEWELS
*From a painted
funeral vase*

BRONZE COVER
FOR A MIRROR
450–400 B.C.

ing round pendant earrings, for well-to-do women delighted in jewelry. Even on tombstones and funeral vases Athenian ladies were pictured looking over their jewels and deciding what to wear!

The Greeks cared little for gems, which were scarce in those days, but they had always loved to deck themselves in gold and silver, and the artists who made bronze mirrors and statuettes could work miracles with precious metals.

123

THE ART OF THE JEWELER

Any citizen of Athens would have been proud to wear this lovely wreath of myrtle, with leaves of thinly beaten silver and stems of slender silver wire.

Wreaths of real leaves, as we have seen, were prizes for athletes at the games, but men also wore them on festive occasions. They favored myrtle wreaths for parties, for these were supposed to chase away the fumes of wine and keep a man clearheaded; and besides, the myrtle was sacred to Aphrodite. Wreaths of ivy were also popular, for the ivy was sacred to

Dionysos. Laurel belonged to Apollo and oak to Zeus, and the olive, created by Athena, was naturally her own special tree.

The exquisite wreaths of gold and silver, made by the goldsmiths, were generally too fragile to be worn. They were intended to serve as offerings at tombs or temples, and they were often buried with the dead.

Necklaces and earrings were for women's delight. This gold necklace, strung with rich rosettes, pointed flower buds and miniature heads, was made in the Greek city of Tarentum in southern Italy, but the ladies of Athens probably had necklaces as splendid.

Their earrings ranged from simple round ones to pendants of infinitely complicated design, such as this little golden ship with scallop shells dangling from it on the thinnest of chains. Aboard the ship a winged siren is perched—one of those mythical birdlike creatures whose irresistible songs, far out at sea, lured unsuspecting sailors to their deaths.

PENDANT
EARRING
5th century B.C.

IMPRESSIONS OF
SEAL STONES
(ENLARGED)
*6th, 5th and 4th
centuries* B.C.

Rings were for men as well as women. Some were made of plain gold, but many were set with seal stones.

Far back in the days before the Greeks had an alphabet—before the ninth century B.C.—the stamp of a man's seal had served as his signature. By the fifth century seal stones were more for decoration than for practical use, treasured for their wonderful designs, each one distinct and different. Whether it was a grazing deer, a charging boar, a man with a bow and arrow or a lion attacking a bull, the design would be beautifully composed in the oval shape of the sliced stone; and the artists of these tiny works took the same delight in animals and men as the carvers of the Parthenon frieze.

But their task was even more difficult than carving in marble. Their designs were not worked in relief but cut into the hard stone in intaglio, like a pattern on a butter mold. Each seal stone took many days of labor. With tiny metal-tipped drills dipped in water and sand, the craftsman gradually ground away the stone to hollow out the design, which is often so small it can be appreciated only through a magnifying glass!

The skilled carvers of gems might also be designers of coins, and cut the dies that stamped the patterns on the metal. Here, there was much work for them to do, for every Greek city of any importance minted its own coinage. In their shops around the Agora of Athens the merchants handled coins from cities all over the Greek world, and some were truly works of art.

SEAL STONE
WITH FIGURE
OF AN ARCHER
(ACTUAL SIZE)
590–490 B.C.

SEAL STONE WITH
LION DESIGN
MOUNTED ON
A GOLD RING
5th–4th century B.C.

127

COINS FROM NEAR AND FAR

An Athenian going shopping in the Agora might carry in his purse ten different sizes of silver coins minted in his own city, from tiny pieces no bigger than a baby's thumbnail to the noble ten-drachma coin above.

This fine coin was minted to celebrate the Greek victory over the Persians at Marathon. Like the sixth-century coins of Athens, it bears the head of Athena on one side and her little owl on the reverse; but now Athena's helmet is adorned with a wreath of upright olive leaves, and her owl has spread his wings in triumph.

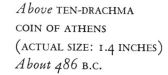

Above TEN-DRACHMA
COIN OF ATHENS
(ACTUAL SIZE: 1.4 INCHES)
About 486 B.C.

128

TEN-DRACHMA COIN OF SYRACUSE
(ACTUAL SIZE: 1.5 INCHES) *479* B.C.

Another famous coin commemorating a victory was made in
the great Greek city of Syracuse in Sicily. Stamped on one side
are a chariot and horses, with a running lion below and a winged
figure of Victory flying above. On the other side is a beautiful
head of Artemis Arethusa, the patron goddess of the city, surrounded by dolphins. The coin was issued after the king of
Syracuse had smashed an invasion by the Phoenicians from
Carthage in North Africa, at about the same time that the
Athenians had beaten back the last Persian invasion of Greece.

After the threat of the Persians was past and Athens had
become the center of an empire, trade was brisk in the Agora,
and the port of Piraeus was busy with ships from the Greek
islands and the distant cities overseas. Many of the ships would
be unloading tall earthenware jars of wine, especially the vessels
from Rhodes.

129

RHODIAN WINE JAR

This coin of Rhodes is stamped with a dramatic head of the sun-god Helios. On the reverse is a budding rose, the symbol of the island, and a tiny sphinx that reminds us of the little sphinxes we saw on the ancient Rhodian jewelry.

SILVER COIN
OF RHODES
About 408 B.C.

From the great island of Crete, to the south, comes a coin bearing heads of Dionysos and Hermes, while the one-drachma

SILVER COIN
OF SYBRITA IN CRETE
About 360 B.C.

SILVER COIN
OF MASSALIA
About 350 B.C.

piece stamped with a benevolent-looking lion and a head of Artemis was made in the Greek city of Massalia (Marseilles), far away to the west.

130

MERCHANTS WEIGHING GRAIN
From a painted vase

Even on the extreme eastern border of the Greek world—
the Crimean peninsula jutting into the Black Sea—coins were
minted with Greek designs. On the back of this one we see
that familiar Eastern monster the griffin, but on the front is the
shaggy head of Silenus, one of the companions of Dionysos in
Greek mythology.

GOLD COIN OF
PANTICAPAEUM
ON THE BLACK SEA
About 380 B.C.

Nothing shows us so clearly as a handful of coins how far
Greek ideas and Greek art had traveled with the adventurers
and merchants of Greece, and how firmly they had taken root
in distant lands with the colonists sent out by the Greek cities.
Then, in the fourth century B.C., with the force of an explosion,
the whole world of Greece was changed.

The old boundaries were burst open, not by the Greeks themselves but by a man from Macedon, a neighboring country that
the Greeks despised as barbaric.

131

BATTLE SCENE *From the Alexander Sarcophagus, 325–300 B.C.*

Philip, king of Macedon, was a fervent admirer of Greek culture and ideas, and when he set out on a career of conquest, he began with Greece. One by one, he subdued the Greek cities until in 338 B.C. he defeated the armies of Athens and Thebes, and the land lay helpless before him. Two years later, Philip was murdered, and his brilliant son Alexander seized the throne of Greece. Vowing to finish what his father had begun, Alexander led his army eastward to challenge the all-powerful empire of Persia and to found a Greek empire reaching to the ends of the earth.

IV TO THE ENDS OF
THE EARTH

PORTRAITS OF MEN AND GODS

By his vision and his ruthless courage, Alexander of Macedon changed the world.

The proud empire of the Persians, which had been for so long a deadly threat to Greece, was crushed at last, and Alexander's conquering army swept on to seize the lands of Asia as far as the river Indus. Alexander founded cities—Greek cities—in the path of his conquests, and spread Greek art and ideas to countries no Greek had ever seen before. He even dreamed of uniting all peoples in a world empire. He did not live to fulfill his dream, but when he died in the year 323 B.C., still a young man, he had already become a hero of legend, and to many people, a god.

After his death his unwieldy empire was split up among different rulers. New cities rose to power and greatness as the capitals of kings, and Athens and the mainland of Greece were no longer the center of the Greek world. Masterpieces of Greek art, like the frieze of carved marble on the next page, were less likely to come from Athens than from the Greek islands or from the cities around the eastern end of the Mediterranean.

The great marble coffin, decorated with this frieze, was found in the royal cemetery at Sidon, a seaport on the Mediterranean coast, in the country now called Lebanon. Who was buried in the coffin is not known, but it was made soon after

COIN OF
ALEXANDER:
HEAD OF
HERAKLES

134

HUNTING SCENE *Part of the frieze of the Alexander Sarcophagus, 325–300 B.C.*

Alexander's death; and the carvings on one side show the conqueror and his army locked in a fierce battle with the Persians. On the other side, hunters on foot and horseback strike down an antlered stag and a furious lion.

The turbulent figures stand out almost in the round, their movement so violent they seem about to burst from the frame. What a contrast to the sculptures of the Parthenon, where even figures in movement seemed calm and controlled!

135

One of the most famous of all Greek statues is the Winged Victory of Samothrace, made in the second century B.C. by a sculptor of Rhodes. The Rhodians were well known as seafarers and sea-fighters, and this statue, set up on the island of Samothrace, was their offering in gratitude for the naval victories of Rhodes over the forces of the king of Syria.

The goddess stands on the stone-carved bow of a ship, bracing herself against the tearing wind, with her great wings spread wide for balance. Even with the head and arms broken away, the figure is thrilling in its power and energy, and the twist of the body and the swirling rhythms of the robe make it exciting to see from any angle, not just from the front.

The sculptors of this time were bold and daring. They wanted to express in bronze and marble what had never been expressed before. They were interested not only in the ideal figures of heroes, gods and goddesses; they also looked keenly at the people of the world around them, all the varied people who walked the streets of the Greek towns, and they began to portray what they saw, rather than simply what they believed to be beautiful.

WINGED VICTORY
OF SAMOTHRACE
About 190 B.C.

BRONZE
JOCKEY
2nd century B.C.

An old woman plodding to market with her chickens and basket of fruit was as interesting to the artist as a winged goddess. He made her wrinkled and worn and worried, as she really was.

For the first time, too, the sculptors showed real children, not looking like small editions of grownups. The little boy in a cloak and the vigorous jockey, scraggy as any street urchin, must have been modeled from life. The jockey's bronze horse is gone, but we can easily picture it, neck outstretched, at full gallop, as the boy leans forward to urge it on.

BRONZE BOY
IN A CLOAK

138

MARBLE STATUE OF AN OLD WOMAN *2nd century* B.C.

Even the young god Eros is shown in this bronze sculpture as a fat sleeping baby, just like a mortal child except for his wings.

BRONZE FIGURE OF EROS ASLEEP 250–150 B.C.

Sculptors in clay, mainly in the Greek town of Tanagra, specialized in making small figures from everyday life, such as the fashionable lady and the little boy in cloak and hat, who might be on his way to school. Like the actor-figures that we have seen, these were made in molds and gaily painted and were meant to be ornaments for people's houses, rather than offerings at temples or tombs.

140

The people of different races, who mingled with the Greeks in the cities of the empire, were not forgotten either. Here we see the head of a shy little Negro girl, and over the page, a brilliant portrait in bronze of a Berber tribesman from North Africa.

Above PAINTED CLAY FIGURES
3rd century B.C.
Right TINY BRONZE JUG
IN THE SHAPE OF A HEAD
300–100 B.C.

BRONZE HEAD OF BERBER TRIBESMAN
4th century B.C.

The sculptors excelled at portraits, in stone, metal and clay, and some of the finest were the miniature portraits on coins.

We have seen how Greek coins often bore on one side the head of a god or a hero. Those issued by Alexander the Great were stamped with the profile of Herakles, but after Alexander's death coins appeared with his own portrait, showing him as the god that many people believed him to be. Then, in Egypt, the first coins were made bearing the portrait of a living ruler—this striking head of the king of Egypt, Ptolemy I.

The idea of issuing coins had spread throughout the lands that Alexander had conquered. Each ruler in the Greek Empire

142

began to mint his own coins, often following Ptolemy's lead and stamping the money with a portrait of himself. From the distant land of Bactria in Central Asia come the best of all these portrait coins, in which we see the faces of the Bactrian rulers, strong, blunt and determined, as they were in life.

COINS OF BACTRIA:
Left EUTHYDEMUS I
226–190 B.C.
Below DEMETRIUS I
190–162 B.C.

Craftsmen who cut the dies for such coins as these and could even carve, in intaglio, amazing portraits on gems, could create exquisite jewelry too. Alexander's empire was immeasurably rich in gold, and there were new precious stones to work with from the conquered East. The task of the jeweler was more important than ever, and a greater challenge to the craftsman's skill, imagination and spirit of adventure.

COIN OF
PTOLEMY I
OF EGYPT
304–285 B.C.

143

GOLD SPIRAL ARMBANDS
3rd century B.C.

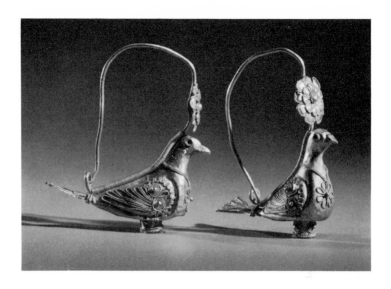

TREASURES OF KINGS AND QUEENS

These splendid spiral armbands are jewelry fit for a queen. Delicately worked in shining gold, they are in the form of mythical creatures of the sea—the fishtailed triton and his tritoness, each of them carrying a tiny baby Eros. They have the same energy as much larger sculptures, and the twist of their bodies is carried right through the lively spirals of their long scaly tails, designed to fit around the arms of the wearer.

A real sea creature, the playful dolphin of the Mediterranean, was a favorite with the makers and wearers of jewelry. It was a symbol of the sea-god Poseidon and also of Aphrodite, the goddess born from the sea. Here, the dolphin's pliant body is shaped into a tiny pendant earring, made of thin sheets of gold with a lacy network of scales laid on in twists of golden wire.

Doves belonged to Aphrodite too. The lovely earrings in the form of doves are made, like the dolphin, of thin gold, with

145

DOLPHIN EARRING
3rd–2nd century B.C.

the feathers outlined in wire. Each bird even has a wire collar around its neck with a hanging golden rosette!

Besides earrings, finger rings and bracelets, a well-dressed lady would wear on her head a golden diadem like a small crown. Around her neck would be a necklace of gold beads, or sometimes beads of glass and garnet, the favorite stone among the jewels from the East.

NECKLACE OF
GLASS AND GARNET BEADS
AND GOLD BRACELET
4th–3rd century B.C.

The cutters of gems, who still made seal stones with miniature designs in intaglio, had discovered a new art—the making of cameos. For this they used stones such as the sardonyx, which is made up of layers of different colors, usually brown and

146

white. A skilled craftsman could cut his design in relief in the top layer of white stone and carve around it just deeply enough to show the lower layer of brown. Then the design would stand out, white and shining, against the dark background.

Many cameos were too large to be worn in rings or necklaces and must have been set in royal crowns or used to decorate metal drinking cups and vases for the tables of the rich. Beautiful vases of gold and bronze had taken the place of the fine painted pottery of former days. Most pottery now was fired in plain black or red, and for people who could not afford vessels of bronze or gold, the potters shaped their vases to look like the metal ones.

Artists who in the past would have been painting vases worked instead on large wall paintings in rich men's houses. Wealthy people lived in far more comfort and luxury than in the old days in Greece. With their splendid jewelry they wore clothes of soft, transparent silk, scented with perfumes from the East. Their meals were flavored with Eastern spices, and their rooms were adorned with carpets and draperies and fine furniture.

They wanted the cities they lived in to be beautiful too, and this was an exciting time for the planning of new cities and the enrichment of old ones with buildings of royal grandeur.

THE HEART OF THE CITY

Alexander the Great had set the example in the founding and building of cities, and the kings who followed him, as rulers of his divided empire, planned their cities to be works of art.

They did not think of towns as simply collections of buildings where people lived and worked and played; they thought of the effect of the whole town, and of the views along its streets from one building to another.

Some of the new cities were seaports, like Alexandria in Egypt, the most famous city founded by Alexander himself. Antioch in Syria, on the other hand, lay along the banks of a river, while Pergamum in Asia Minor was perched high on

148

a hilltop, with streets and buildings piled in dizzying terraces.

Whatever their setting, the new towns were usually planned with straight streets crossing at right angles, instead of wandering about like footpaths, as they did in older towns. The streets were not often paved, but the cities were kept clean, and good supplies of water were piped from reservoirs or big cisterns to the public fountains, where women came to fill their tall water jars.

Besides houses for the citizens, every town needed one or more temples, a theater, a town hall and a gymnasium for athletics. Most important of all was the open market place, the Agora, flanked by long covered colonnades called *stoas,* where people could walk and talk and do their shopping.

The Agora of Athens, as we have seen, had been for cen-

turies the heart of the city's life. Far more than a market and a center of government and law courts, the Agora was a holy place too, where no one dared disturb the peace. Temples and altars were built there, and the Temple of Hephaistos, god of the craftsmen, still stands today on its small hill overlooking the Agora.

The days of Athens' power were gone, but the old city was not neglected in this time of new building. The kings of the Greek Empire still respected Athens as the fountain of ideas, a place of deep learning and wonderful art. King Attalos II of Pergamum was a special friend of the city, and in the second century B.C. he presented Athens with a handsome building for the Agora. It was a stoa of impressive size, which closed in the whole eastern side of the old market place. At right angles to it was the new South Stoa, and between them ran the Processional Way to the Acropolis.

Today, when all the ancient buildings of the Agora, except for the Temple of Hephaistos, can be seen only as foundations, the Stoa of Attalos has been rebuilt as it was. Here we can walk

150

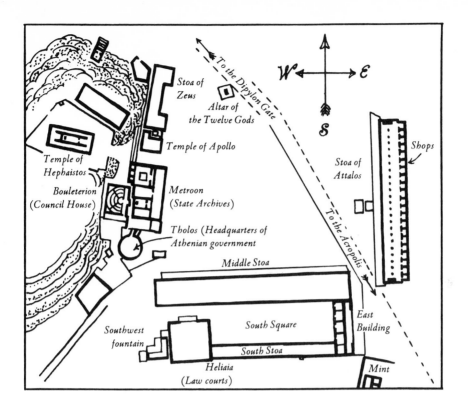

as the Greeks walked in the second century B.C., when the building was new, and find shade and coolness from the morning sun and shelter from the rain under the great colonnade.

The small rooms behind the pillared porch were designed to be shops, with tall square-cut doorways; and on the floor above were offices and another porch, a fine vantage point for watching parades along the Processional Way or simply for gazing on all the bustle of the market. Down in the bright sunshine would be market women and craftsmen and sellers of flowers and wreaths; loads of wine jars on creaking wagons; philosophers and politicians at their endless arguments, with young men eagerly listening; poets reciting verses, slaves running errands and merchants striking a bargain; and beyond and above it all,

up the Processional Way, the serene and perfect beauty of the Parthenon on its high, rocky hill.

Here below the Acropolis, with the potters' quarter and the ancient cemetery not far away, we are back where we started in the eighth century B.C., when Athens was a small and unimportant place, but alive with new ideas.

In the second century B.C., soon after the Stoa of Attalos was built, Athens and all Greece were conquered by the rising power of Rome. A new age began, in which Greece was only a part of the vast Roman Empire. But the spirit of Greek art, born in Athens, did not die. It conquered Rome.

THE TRIUMPH OF

GREEK ART

The Roman conquerors gazed at the Greek temples and sculptures with amazement and delight. Shiploads of Greek statues were carried off to Italy, and rich Romans ordered hundreds of copies of them, carved in marble, to adorn their villas.

Many centuries later, these copies of Greek statues were rediscovered by the great artists of the Italian Renaissance, who brought about a rebirth of Greek art. Artists and architects traveled to Greece to see for themselves, and even to take away, Greek statues and "antiquities." Greek ideas of art spread across the world, throughout Europe and over the Atlantic to America.

Men used those ideas in ways that would have astonished the Greeks—in grandiose paintings and sculptures, and in the building of churches and town halls and country houses. If we look about, we can see echoes of Greek art all around us, faint imitations that too often seem dry and dead.

But the true art of Greece was full of life and strength and joy. Today, although the Greek temples have been shattered by wars and earthquakes, the statues broken and so much lost forever, Greek art still lives on in all its richness, to inspire us once again, and for always, with the Greeks' exciting vision of men and gods.

153

LIST OF ILLUSTRATIONS

Photographs

154

Drawings   (location of objects shown in drawings)

BOOKS FOR FURTHER READING

Barron, John. *Greek Sculpture*. New York: E. P. Dutton & Co., Inc. (A Dutton/Vista Pictureback), 1965.

Boardman, John. *Greek Art*. New York: Frederick A. Praeger (Praeger World of Art Paperback), 1964.

——.*The Greeks Overseas*. Harmondsworth, England: Penguin Books, 1964.

Charbonneaux, Jean. *Greek Bronzes*. New York: The Viking Press, Inc., 1962.

Cook, Robert M. *The Greeks Until Alexander*. New York: Frederick A. Praeger (*Ancient Peoples and Places* series), 1962.

Corbett, P. E. *The Sculpture of the Parthenon*. Harmondsworth, England: Penguin Books, 1959.

Finley, Moses I. *The Ancient Greeks*. New York: The Viking Press, Inc. (Compass Books), 1964.

Hamilton, Edith. *Mythology*. New York: New American Library (Mentor Books), 1964.

Lane, Arthur. *Greek Pottery*. London: Faber and Faber Ltd., 1948.

Rose, H. J. *Gods and Heroes of the Greeks*. Cleveland and New York: The World Publishing Company (Meridian Books), 1958.

Seltman, Charles. *Approach to Greek Art*. New York: E. P. Dutton & Co., Inc. (A Dutton Paperback), 1960.

——. *A Book of Greek Coins*. Harmondsworth, England: Penguin Books, 1950.

Webster, T.B.L. *Greek Terracottas*. Harmondsworth, England: Penguin Books, 1950.

(Also guidebooks and picture books published by The British Museum, The Metropolitan Museum of Art, the Museum of Fine Arts, Boston, and the American School of Classical Studies at Athens.)